P. M.

# *The Grandchildren of the*
# VIKINGS

# THE WORLD'S CHILDREN

# The Grandchildren of the
# VIKINGS

MATTI A. PITKÄNEN

WITH REIJO HÄRKÖNEN

Carolrhoda Books, Inc./Minneapolis

This edition first published 1996 by Carolrhoda Books, Inc.
First published in Finland in 1989 by Otava Publishing Company Ltd.
under the title VIIKINKIEN JÄLKELÄISET.
Original edition copyright © 1989 by Matti A. Pitkänen
Additional text copyright © 1996 by Carolrhoda Books, Inc.

Carolrhoda Books, Inc. c/o The Lerner Group
241 First Avenue North, Minneapolis, MN 55401

LIBRARY OF CONGRESS CATALOGING-IN-PUBLICATION DATA

Pitkänen, Matti A.
  [Viikinkien jälkeläiset.  English]
  The grandchildren of the vikings / Matti A. Pitkänen with Reijo Härkönen.
    p. cm. — (World's children)
  Includes index.
  ISBN 0-87614-889-5 (lib. bdg.)
  1. Vikings—Juvenile literature. 2. Iceland—Description and travel—Juvenile
literature. 3. Islands—Scandinavia—Description and travel—Juvenile literature.
4. Lofoten (Norway)—Description and travel—Juvenile literature. 5. Gotland
(Sweden)—Description and travel—Juvenile literature. 6. Åland (Finland)—
Description and travel—Juvenile literature. 7. Faroe Islands—Description and
travel—Juvenile literature. [1. Vikings. 2. Iceland—Description and travel.
3. Islands—Scandinavia—Description and travel.] I. Härkönen, Reijo. II. Title.
III. Series.
DL65.P5313  1996
948—dc20                                                             94-38679

Manufactured in the United States of America
1 2 3 4 5 6 – JR – 01  00  99  98  97  96

More than one thousand years ago, graceful wooden ships set out from the shores of what are now Norway, Sweden, and Denmark. These ships were built by people called the Vikings. The time when they lived and sailed their ships, from about the year A.D. 800 to A.D. 1100, is known as the Viking Age.

Although they came from very different parts of Scandinavia, the Vikings shared a common language called Old Norse. They also shared a common goal—to take their ships on voyages of discovery.

Why did they sail away from their homes? The Vikings didn't leave newspapers or diaries behind to tell us. But from other clues—ruins of old settlements, stones carved with pictures, and old stories—we can discover some of the reasons why they left. And we can tell where they went on their travels.

*The bow, or forward end, of a Viking ship*

Even before the year 800, Vikings were traveling far and wide around Europe. Some were farmers who had suffered from bad harvests and bad weather at home. They were hoping to take food in raids or by trading. Some had to leave their homelands because there were too many people for the land to support. They were looking for new, less crowded places to live.

In the Viking Age, many men believed that they had to prove their bravery to their families and home settlements by becoming warriors. These Vikings traveled as far south as Spain and as far east as what is now Russia. They conquered England, took slaves in Ireland, and burned churches in France.

Wherever they went, their name at first frightened the people they met. Even now, when people think of the word *Viking,* they think of fierce and powerful men from the north making bloody raids. But while some Vikings raided and killed, many others settled and lived peacefully in their new homes. The Vikings spent more time trading, farming, and fishing than they did conquering other people. And when they went looking for more places to trade, farm, and fish, they made some incredible discoveries.

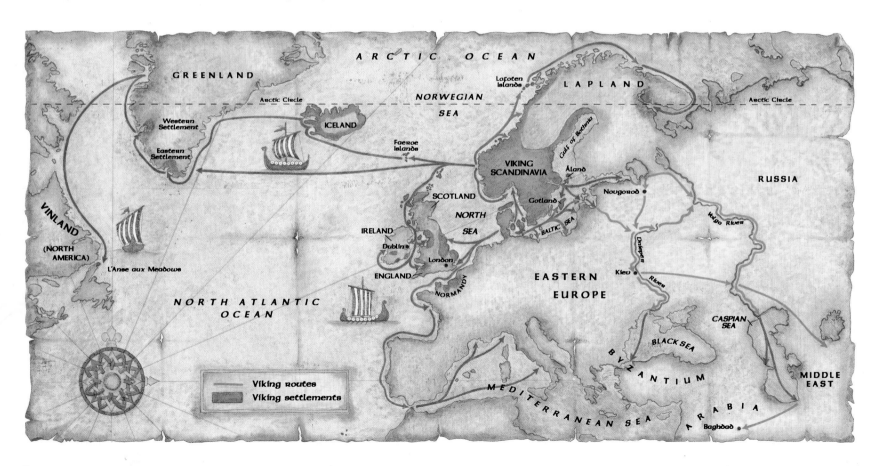

Viking ships traveled far. They had oars for rowing when the winds were calm and sails for catching even the smallest breezes. They were sturdy enough to withstand long voyages at sea but could also travel through narrow bays and shallow rivers. These ships carried the earliest settlers north to Lofoten, an island chain off the coast of Norway, near the Arctic Circle. They came east to Gotland and Åland, islands off the Swedish mainland. And they traveled amazing distances westward to the Faeroe Islands, to Iceland, and to Greenland. Viking boats also landed in a place called Vinland. (Its modern name is North America.)

Not all of the Viking settlements lasted. In Vinland, only the ruins of a few houses in eastern Canada survive to tell us of the Vikings' presence. In Greenland, all the Viking settlers had left or died by 1500. But in the Faeroes, Iceland, Lofoten, Åland, and Gotland today, people in many ways resemble their Viking ancestors. These modern-day inhabitants are the grandchildren of the Vikings.

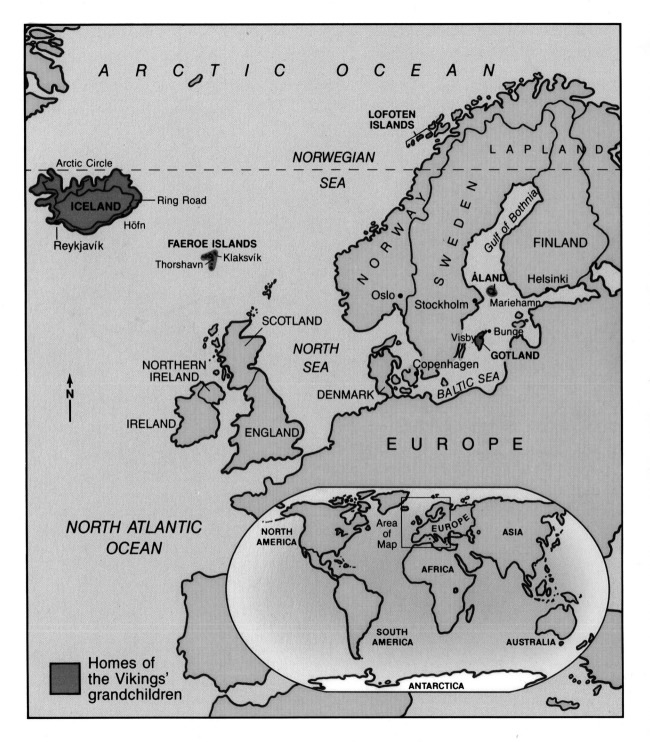

Homes of the Vikings' grandchildren

Above: *Around their shoulders, Berita and Dorita wear Faeroese capes embroidered with their family's own design. They and their friend Bjarni* (opposite page) *wear traditional outfits for special occasions such as boat races, school graduations, and church holidays.*

The Faeroe Islands are closer to Scotland than to Scandinavia, but maps don't tell the whole story. The people of the Faeroes have roots in the Viking Age. Viking explorers from Norway settled these scattered islands in the North Atlantic Ocean in the early 800s. They didn't find any people living on the islands, but they did find sheep. The name *Faeroe* means "island of sheep" in Old Norse.

Berita and Dorita are dressed in their national costumes. It's Sunday, and there's a rowing race in Klaksvík. The two girls will watch the race from the shoreline. Bjarni, their friend, will be watching, too. He's put on his cap—always a good idea in the Faeroes, where the weather can change from one minute to the next. They're all hoping that after the race their parents will take them to the traditional ring dance or to a sheepshearing contest.

For now, all eyes are on the swiftly moving boats. Teams from all of the 17 inhabited islands have been competing in races for hundreds of years. If you look closely, you can see that the ships' design has been handed down, almost unchanged, from Viking times.

Ships helped the Vikings get around in an age when there weren't any airplanes or cars or roads. Now the Faeroe Islands are linked by buses that travel modern roadways and by helicopter routes. But boats are still very useful to the islanders. Small boats are used for fishing just offshore. Larger ships, filled with a catch of deep-sea fish or with tourists, crowd the port at Thorshavn, the capital of the Faeroes.

Top left: *Rowing is still an important skill in the Faeroes, although more and more people use motorized boats and even helicopters to travel from island to island.* Opposite page: *Thorshavn is the Faeroese capital and the largest city in the island group. People call it Havn, or the harbor, for short.*

*The first flowers of spring are a good excuse for Sigrid and Arendur to take a walk in a meadow on the Faeroes.*

*A* tjaldur, *or oystercatcher*

Sigrid and Arendur, like many people on the Faeroes, can trace their families back to the Viking Age. Most of the original Viking settlers came from Norway. The Faeroese still have strong ties to Norway and to Denmark, which ruled the islands for many centuries. The islands are now part of Denmark, but they have their own government, flag, money, and stamps.

They also have their own official bird, the oystercatcher or *tjaldur.* The rugged coastline of the Faeroes is home to oystercatchers, puffins, gulls, and many other seabirds. Continuing a tradition handed down from the Vikings, the Faeroese still hunt along the islands' rocky shores for birds and birds' eggs to eat.

Above: *Steep hills are common on the Faeroes, but that doesn't stop Rógvi from exploring on his bike. Streymoy and the other islands in the Faeroes were formed by a volcanic eruption 50 million years ago. Opposite page: Salt-laden winds from the ocean strip houses of paint, so buildings on the Faeroes must be frequently repainted.*

Rógvi is 12 years old and lives on the main island, Streymoy. He plans to stay on the island after he has finished school. Many young people have gone to Denmark and even farther away to look for work. Rógvi's father fishes for a living, but Rógvi doesn't think he will follow in his father's footsteps. Fishing can be a hard life, with many weeks spent at sea.

In the past, people on the Faeroes caught pilot whales for food, but nowadays the catch is small. Pilot whales are not an endangered species, but many people in other countries and even from within the Faeroes want to stop whale hunting.

Rógvi knows that there are few jobs outside the fishing industry, but he still wants to stay on the Faeroes. As the Faeroese like to tell visitors, the Faeroes are the best islands in all of Europe.

Not long after the Faeroe Islands were settled, Viking boats touched the shoreline of a large and uninhabited land to the north. The Vikings called it *Ísland*, or Iceland, because of the cold and icy appearance of most of the island.

Even though it didn't look or sound very promising, before long Viking settlers and their families had arrived. They were looking for new land to farm. To help out, they brought along farm horses. Those animals are the ancestors of today's Icelandic horses.

Horses were important to the Vikings and to present-day Icelanders as well. For over a thousand years, it has been forbidden to bring foreign breeds of horses to Iceland. In the countryside, children and adults still ride horses into town or to school. School only begins once the horses and sheep have been herded in from their summer pastures.

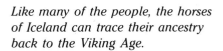

*Like many of the people, the horses of Iceland can trace their ancestry back to the Viking Age.*

When Ingólfur Árnason, Iceland's first settler, arrived in about 870, he saw something smoky rising from the bay where he landed. It was steam from one of Iceland's many hot springs, but Ingólfur Árnason didn't know that. He called the place "Smoky Bay" or Reykjavík. The name stuck, and today it's the site of Iceland's bustling and modern capital city.

Elísa is from Reykjavík. She goes to day care while her parents work. This morning, like many mornings at day care, she heard an old story from Iceland's Viking past. It was part of a *saga*, a story of brave deeds and long journeys from the Viking Age.

Elísa and other Icelanders can understand the *sagas* even though most were written down hundreds of years ago. Icelandic, the language spoken on Iceland, hasn't changed much from Old Norse. Icelandic does, however, have two letters found in no other language: ð and þ.

*Modern Iceland shows its face in buildings and signs in Reykjavík (above and below),* but signs of the past remain. *This stone (right) was carved with runes in the Viking Age.*

Stefán lives in Reykjavík too, but he spends his summers at his grandparents' farm on the north coast of the island. Stefán sometimes herds the cows and sheep, but his grandparents use machines to do nearly all of the farmwork.

This farmland is rich and fertile, but most of the land on Iceland is uninhabitable. There are vast cold deserts, where the land is too dry for anything to grow. There are also fields of sand. All of the usable land is near the coast.

Iceland's unusual landscape comes in part from its many volcanoes. The country has about half a dozen active ones.

*Members of Stefán's family have owned and worked this sheepfarm in northern Iceland for generations.*

In summertime, when school is out, Karl Jónas goes to visit family in Höfn. He loves to fish and play with the sheepdogs, but many other visitors come to the area to see Iceland's natural wonders. Waterfalls, geysers, hot springs, and steaming lava fields left after volcanic eruptions seem normal and ordinary to Karl Jónas.

Icelanders get much of their electricity by harnessing the power of the island's hot springs and geysers. With so much steam heat around, it's surprising that well into summertime Iceland is still quite cold. Icelanders call their country the land of fire and ice. And they say that Iceland has only two seasons, a light one and a dark one. In winter the sun never shines for long, while in summer it lights the sky long into the night. Yet even in June, the ground is often still frozen.

Opposite page: *Fast-flowing waterfalls, steaming lava fields, hot springs, and spouting geysers are just a few of Iceland's natural wonders.* Right: *Karl Jónas*

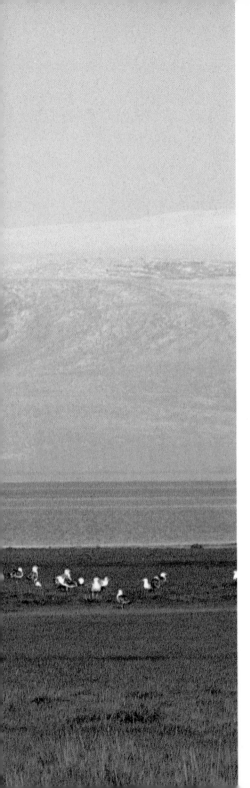

Despite the cold, swans and many other migrating birds come to Iceland to mate, nest, and raise their young. These swans have come back to their old nest, one they have used for years. When their cygnets hatch, the swans will teach their young to swim and to catch insects right away.

Near the swans' nesting place, there is a glacier. One-tenth of Iceland is covered in ancient ice fields. They are slowly melting and shrinking. In summer, massive blocks of ice separate from the glaciers, drop into the sea, and melt.

When the Vikings first settled in Iceland and saw the glaciers, they thought the ice would melt by summer. When it didn't melt, some of the Vikings decided not to stay and set out for a new home. But the glaciers are still here, just as many descendants of the Vikings are.

Right: *Melting glaciers feed the lakes, rivers, and streams of Iceland.*

Left: *A picture stone on Gotland tells a story from the island's Viking past.* Opposite page: *Windmills and ruins dot the flat landscape of Gotland.*

Settlers in the Faeroes and Iceland traveled long distances to their new homes. But the Vikings had to make only a short journey by boat to get from what is now Sweden to Gotland, an island in the Baltic Sea. When they arrived in the 800s, people were already living there. But the original Gotlanders soon made room for Viking settlers.

In Viking times, summer was spent farming. In the winter months, Vikings left their island farms to make trading voyages far to the east. Gold and silver coins from what is now Russia are still being found where Viking traders buried them for safekeeping hundreds of years ago.

But you don't have to dig to find clues to Gotland's Viking past. Picture stones, like this one in Bunge, tell stories of Viking battles and voyages at sea.

Left: *Gunnilla's family lives in Visby, Gotland's largest city. As in all parts of the island, however, they're never far from the beach.*

For short trips on Gotland, a bike is the best way to get around. Gunnilla is on her way to the beach with her mother. The cobblestone streets outside her family's house in Visby make for a bouncy ride. But once outside the walled city, it's smooth sailing.

Gunnilla's rose-covered cottage isn't too far from Pippi Longstocking's home. Pippi is a character created by the Swedish writer Astrid Lindgren. Villekulla Cottage, where Pippi is supposed to have lived, is said to be somewhere on the winding streets of Visby.

Along the shore, steep rocky bluffs alternate with gently sloping beaches. Gotland's sandy shores were good landing places for Viking boats. Now the beaches are a favorite destination for sunbathers.

Many come from mainland Sweden for vacation. Although modern-day Gotland is a province of Sweden, people from the mainland often joke that they feel like they're going to a foreign country when they visit. Some Gotlanders, or *gutarna,* as they call themselves, still speak a traditional dialect. The dialect dates back hundreds of years and in that way is similar to Icelandic.

Right: *Lummelund Cavern.* Below: *Ole and Jan.* Opposite page: Raukar, *limestone rock formations, are common on Gotland.*

Gotland's Viking past isn't the only thing that makes it special. This island is composed almost completely of limestone. Massive rock formations, called *raukar,* cover the landscape in parts of the island.

Limestone caverns and caves are also big attractions. Olle and Jan often visit caves in the north of Gotland. They're ready to start exploring a famous cave with other members of their scout troop from Visby.

In 1950, schoolchildren just about their age were exploring the same cave when rocks shifted. Behind fallen rocks they found the entrance to beautiful Lummelund Cavern, which is at least one and a half miles long.

North of Gotland, between Sweden and Finland, lie the Åland Islands. During Viking times, explorers and traders from Sweden landed here in their swift wooden boats. Even now boats are an important part of life in Åland.

Lena and Inga are taking a tour of the *Pommern,* a four-masted fishing ship that now serves as a museum. High above, a sailor climbs the masts. Belowdecks, Lena and Inga can take turns pretending to nap in a sailor's berth. The *Pommern,* built in 1903, hasn't sailed the waters around these islands for some time, but many other boats come in and out of local harbors. Mariehamn, the largest town in Åland, is also the biggest port.

Like the Faeroes, the Åland Islands are self-governing. They are under the control of Finland, although their people have strong ties to Sweden, dating back to the Viking Age.

*On board the* Pommern, *a museum ship, the fishing and shipping history of the Åland Islands comes alive for Lena and Inga and other visitors.*

Just south of Mariehamn is one of Åland's many meadows. In the warm summer air, nightingales sing, cowslips bloom, and crickets chirp. Gunnar, a young butterfly collector, tries to catch one of the islands' many varieties.

The islands' great natural beauty makes them a favorite stop for nature lovers. The mild climate helps plants and trees grow. Southern hardwoods, such as ash, hazelnut, and oak, thrive in the inland forests.

The name *Åland* means "the land of water." The thousands of islands, skerries, shoals, and shallows that make up the Åland Islands are unique in the world.

It's hard to believe that 11,000 years ago, these islands were covered with ice from great glaciers. The land rose slowly from the sea, and the glaciers receded. The land is still rising a little over half a yard every 100 years.

The first settlers came to Åland to fish, and fishing remains a major industry. It's also one of Annika's favorite things to do. Each summer Annika's cousins come to visit from Sweden. Annika and her cousin Mikael put out nets in Djupvik. Now they're taking in a morning catch of flatfish. The fish will be smoked before it's eaten.

Annika's cousins aren't the only summer visitors to Åland. Ferryboats from Sweden and Finland keep the islands connected to the mainland all year-round. In summer, they bring in loads of tourists.

*While the midsummer sun shines into the evening, villagers raise flower-covered poles throughout Åland.*

On the Åland Islands, old traditions live on. Each year at midsummer, elaborate poles, a bit like maypoles, are set up in each village. The whole village shares in decorating the pole with flowers, colored ribbons, and miniature boats and ships. Some people even decorate themselves to celebrate the season.

In the evening, while bonfires burn over the islands, people dance and sing around the pole. Even after the celebration is over, the pole stays standing. It will stay there as a reminder of summer until the next Midsummer Eve.

Miles away from Åland, off the northern shores of Norway, Ivar celebrates summer by sitting in the warm sun on a pier in Lofoten. Although this group of islands is best known for winter fishing, you'll find cod drying on wooden racks in the harbors through early summer.

You'll also find plenty of birds in Lofoten. On Værøy, one of the islands in the group, the thousands of puffins, terns, and other seabirds more than outnumber the 900 or so people who live there.

Left: *Ivar.* Opposite page: *A fishing boat* (above left) *lies surrounded by cast nets, while an earlier day's catch of cod dries on open-air racks* (above right) *in a harbor in Lofoten. Known as* tørrfisk, *the cod dries from late winter until the following June.*

Left: *The islands in the Lofoten chain rise up steeply from the ocean. Seen from a distance, they look like a single, unbroken range and are sometimes called the Lofoten Wall.*

Lofoten is made up of many islands in the North Atlantic Ocean. There are valleys and bogs, plains and sandy beaches, along with tall mountain ranges. No matter where you are in Lofoten, you're always close to water.

Indoor swimming pools are in constant use. In Lofoten, it's important to know how to swim well. Dangerous sea currents flow between the islands. Between the islands of Moskenes and Værøy there is a whirlpool, with the power to destroy even large ships.

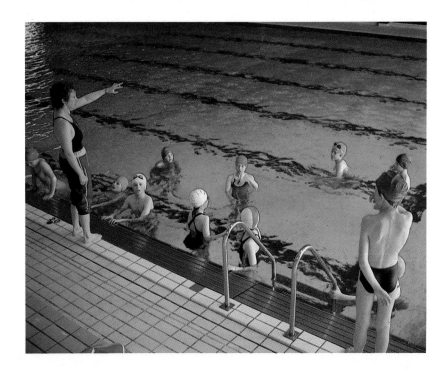

Left: *Once used by the Vikings to sail the waters around Lofoten, this well-preserved ship now serves as a reminder of the area's past.*

The Vikings safely skirted the whirlpool when they came to Lofoten in the 800s. They were drawn to these islands for fishing in the coastal waters. Staying at first just for the winter fish harvest, they eventually built homes, farmed, and raised families year-round.

Nowadays, only ruins remain of the farms they built. One such ruin, on the island of Vestvågøy, was the home of a Viking chief. He died over one thousand years ago, but it's likely that some of today's islanders are related to him.

As in many other places settled by the Vikings, reminders of the past linger on. You'll see them not just in Lofoten, but also on the Faeroes, Iceland, Gotland, and Åland. You'll see history's traces in the way people live their lives, in their favorite traditions, and in the faces of the modern-day inhabitants—the grandchildren of the Vikings.

## Glossary

*Faeroe:* island of sheep
*gutarna:* Gotlanders, in the dialect of Gotland
*Ísland:* the Viking name for Iceland
*raukar:* freestanding limestone formations
*runes:* characters in the alphabet used by the Vikings
*saga:* an Icelandic tale of historic or legendary events recorded hundreds of years ago
*tjaldur:* the official bird of the Faeroes, known in English as the oystercatcher
*tørrfisk:* dried cod

## Pronunciation Guide

**Åland**  OH-lahnd
**Faeroes**  FEHR-ohz
**Gotland**  GAWT-lahnd
**Lofoten**  LOH-foh-tuhn
**Mariehamn**  muh-ree-HAMN
**Reykjavík**  RAY-kyuh-vihk
**saga**  SAH-guh
**Thorshavn**  TORSH-hown
**tørrfisk**  TER-fisk

# Index